Part 2

The **Feast** _of_

Wisdom

More Biblical Answers To Common Questions That Deepen Your Faith

COLETTE A. GUTHRIE

PUBLISHERS

ISBN: 978-1-966723-18-9 (paperback)

ACKNOWLEDGMENTS

To Coach Crystal Daye, thank you for sparking the idea for this book.

To the Kencot Seventh-day Adventist Church's Personal Ministries team, thanks for giving me the opportunity to write Bible lessons for Revelation seminars.

To all my friends who have asked me Bible questions, thank you.

TABLE OF CONTENTS

INTRODUCTION

In *The Feast of Wisdom - Part 1*, I shared my experiences of going to the public library to read books, primarily fiction.

I attended a boarding school for my seven high school years. In high school, the main objective of going to the library was to get assignments done. Encyclopaedias were my favourites! The World Wide Web was born in the late 1980s—around the time I started high school. Consequently, I was not then exposed to this method of conducting research.

At university, visits to the library were primarily for conducting research. We relied on paper books and sometimes were challenged by the scarcity of key books. Some material was available in microfiche format, but I never accessed it.

The birth of artificial intelligence has taken online research to dizzying heights while presenting a significant challenge to information accuracy and credibility as the level of attention to detail of the information found on the internet can vary widely. In addition, information found online can change or disappear frequently. This has serious implications for those relying solely on the Internet for Bible study.

While the Bible is a constant, unchanging guide, given to help us navigate the uncertain times in which we live, we need to have strong Bible study skills to get correct answers to the important questions of faith.

My primary goal for *The Feast of Wisdom - Part 2* is to equip Bible students with the skills needed to answer their key questions of faith through a careful study of several verses in the Scriptures with emphasis on Ecclesiastes. Interesting lessons from the culinary world are sprinkled throughout the book.

ABOUT THE BIBLE

- The Bible is a collection of 66 books in one binding.

- About 40 different authors wrote the Bible over a period of 1500 years.

- Each Bible writer wrote in his native language—Hebrew, Aramaic, or Greek.

- These writers came from various backgrounds, different levels of education, and different cultures.

- Scripture is not the thoughts and ideas of these individual men: *"for prophecy never came by the will of man, but holy men of God spoke as they were moved by the Holy Spirit." (2 Peter 1:21 –NKJV).*

BIBLE STUDY PRINCIPLES

"Study to shew thyself approved unto God, a workman that needeth not to be ashamed, rightly dividing the word of truth." (2 Timothy 2:15 – KJV).

It is important to follow the following principles when reading and studying the Bible:

1. **Always ask** for the guidance of the Holy Spirit before studying the Bible because the Bible is the inspired Word of God.

2. **Approach** Bible study with an attitude of humility and an open mind, seeking to learn, never with preconceived ideas nor with pride of opinion.

3. **Ask** questions as you read and study, and diligently seek the answers.

4. **Apply** all Scripture passages or verses on a topic in order to clarify a subject.

5. **Amplify** the meaning of words through the use of tools such as a Strong's concordance, Hebrew and Greek dictionaries, Bible commentaries, and computer programs. All these will greatly enhance our studies.

6. **Ascertain** the context of a passage. A passage is a group of verses. We must be careful not to take one or more verses out of their "context" and use them to teach something unrelated to the subject matter of the passage.

7. **Allow** the Bible to interpret itself rather than depending on speculation and guesswork.

8. **Acquaint** yourself with Jesus—a personal, intimate relationship with Him is the main aim of Bible study.

9. *Apparent* **discrepancies** may often be explained by a careful study of the entire Bible, comparing verse with verse so that all the available evidence is obtained rather than looking at only one or two verses and possibly drawing the wrong conclusions.

10. **Allow** yourself enough time to study the Bible for yourself. A superficial reading of the Bible will only result in a superficial understanding of the Bible.

MORE ABOUT ECCLESIASTES

"The words of the wise are like [prodding] goads, and these collected sayings are [firmly fixed in the mind] like well-driven nails; they are given by one Shepherd." (Ecclesiastes 12:11 - AMP).

Let's explore the elements in Ecclesiastes 12:11.

- *The Goads:* A goad was a stick with nails on it to make an animal move from its comfortable position to a place desired by the livestock manager, perhaps to a place with better grazing. The words of wise men are like goads in that they prod us to leave our comfort zones as God directs. They are guiding lights.[1]

- *Collected Sayings:* Some *wise men*, like Solomon the Preacher, are able to skillfully combine multiple proverbs into helpful instruction. These collections provide a compelling and reliable basis for successful living.[2]

- *Well-driven Nails*: In the same way that well-driven nails hold a house together, words of wisdom are like well-driven nails that make all aspects of our lives fit together properly.[3]

- *One Shepherd*: As Israel's king, Solomon was charged with shepherding God's chosen nation (see 2 Samuel 5:2). As a work of wisdom, Ecclesiastes demonstrates that Solomon was exceptionally qualified to govern the nation of Israel as

---

[1] "The Bible Says, Ecclesiastes 12:11-12 Meaning"
https://thebiblesays.com/en/commentary/ecc+12:11
[2] Ibid
[3] Ibid

13

its God-appointed shepherd and to provide the insights in this book.[4]

THE LESSON

Solomon got wisdom as a gift from God (see 1 Kings 3:12). Solomon's collections let us know that if we want to succeed in life, we do not need to go beyond what God has written in His Word. Like sharp goads, the wisdom found in the Word should guide our choices.

"For the word of God is living and powerful, and sharper than any two-edged sword, piercing even to the division of soul and spirit, and of joints and marrow, and is a discerner of the thoughts and intents of the heart." (Hebrews 4:12 - NKJV).

THE TAKEAWAY

The source of all wisdom is God, the Shepherd of our souls (see 1 Peter 2:25). Pursue wisdom but trust God to guide, nourish, and protect you from going astray as you feed on His Word.

---

[4] Ibid

REJOICE ...

"... eat ... drink ... be merry ..."
(Ecclesiastes 8:15 - KJV).

Twice As Nice

"As thou knowest not what is the way of the spirit, nor how the bones do grow in the womb of her that is with child: even so thou knowest not the works of God who maketh all." (Ecclesiastes 11:5 - KJV).

DID YOU KNOW?

- Fried ice cream or tempura ice cream is a dessert made of a scoop of ice cream that is frozen hard, then breaded or coated in a batter before being quickly deep-fried, creating a warm, crispy shell around the still-cold ice cream. It is common in Chinese and Mexican cuisine.

- The dessert is commonly made by taking a scoop of ice cream frozen well below the temperature at which ice cream is generally kept, possibly coating it in raw egg, rolling it in cornflakes or cookie crumbs, and briefly deep frying it. The extremely low temperature of the ice cream prevents it from melting while being fried.

- It may be sprinkled with cinnamon and sugar and a touch of peppermint, though whipped cream or honey may be used as well.[5]

CHILDHOOD MEMORIES

Many of my childhood memories include my mom's homemade ice cream. It was customary to have ice cream at our small birthday gatherings when we got together to toast each celebrant.

---

[5] https://en.wikipedia.org/wiki/Fried_ice_cream

I also remember learning and singing the song "Children Learn What They Live" in the choir in my first year in high school. The chorus of the song went like this:

"Children learn what they live
Children live what they learn
Teach them the way to love in their hearts
And they will find love in the world."[6]

Little did I know that the words of the stanzas of the song were taken from an inspirational poem of the same name, written by Dorothy Law Nolte—parent, educator, and family counsellor. Published in 1954, about 30 years after her birth, it was pasted to refrigerators, printed on posters, and distributed to millions of parents by a baby formula maker.[7]

Let us explore the topic of baptism.

1. What is baptism?

" ... Philip said, If thou believest with all thine heart, thou mayest. And he answered and said, I believe that Jesus Christ is the Son of God." (Acts 8:37 - KJV).

According to Smith's Bible Dictionary, baptism is *"the public profession of faith and discipleship."*[8] It is done as a statement of one's confession of faith in Christ—belief in and acceptance of the truth about Jesus: His life, death, and resurrection. The Ethiopian

---

[6] YouTube Video: Love (Children Learn What They Live)
https://youtu.be/UTYi2hdZ8N8?si=YbpASqpqNVInFV62
[7] "Children Learn What They Live: Lessons From Dorothy Law Nolte",
https://www.rootsofaction.com/children-learn-what-they-live-lessons-from-dorothy-law-nolte/
[8] https://www.kingjamesbibledictionary.com/Dictionary/baptism

eunuch was baptised as a result of his belief that Jesus was the Son of God.

2. *What is a prerequisite for baptism?*

" And Philip ran thither to him, and heard him read the prophet Esaias, and said, Understandest thou what thou readest? Then Philip opened his mouth, and began at the same scripture, and preached unto him Jesus." (Acts 8:30,35 - KJV).

Before anyone is baptized, they should have a biblical understanding of the truth about Jesus.

3. *What is the significance of baptism?*

"And now why tarriest thou? arise, and be baptized, and wash away thy sins, calling on the name of the Lord." (Acts 22:16 - KJV).

Baptism signifies cleansing or washing someone from sin. It represents an integral part of the process of salvation (see Mark 16:16).

4. *What is the biblical method of baptism?*

" ... Jesus, when he was baptized, went up straightway out of the water: and, lo, the heavens were opened unto him, and he saw the Spirit of God descending like a dove, and lighting upon him." (Matthew 3:16 - KJV).

Jesus was baptised by John the Baptist in the River Jordan as an example for us to follow. Throughout the Bible, we see that baptism was by immersion of the whole person in much water (see the example of Philip baptising the eunuch in Acts 8:36, 38).

5. *What does the biblical method of baptism symbolise?*

"Buried with him in baptism, wherein also ye are risen with him through the faith of the operation of God, who hath raised him from the dead." (Colossians 2:12 - KJV).

Baptism by immersion symbolises death to sin, burial of the old man and his ways of sin, and resurrection to new life in righteousness.

6. *What is the place of baptism in the Christian community?*

"Go ye therefore, and teach all nations, baptizing them in the name of the Father, and of the Son, and of the Holy Ghost." (Matthew 28:19 - KJV).

The command to baptize was coextensive with the command to preach the gospel. All nations were to be evangelised; and they were to be made disciples, admitted into the fellowship of Christ's religion by baptism.

7. *What gift do believers receive at baptism?*

"Then Peter said unto them, Repent, and be baptized every one of you in the name of Jesus Christ for the remission of sins, and ye shall receive the gift of the Holy Ghost." (Acts 2:38 - KJV).

The Holy Spirit is present throughout the process of salvation, convicting sinners of sin, of righteousness, and of judgment as they read the Scriptures, helping individuals to enter into a new spiritual reality and empowering believers in Jesus to live righteously in this world until Jesus returns (see Titus 2:11-13).

THE LESSON

As strange as it seems, fried ice cream is an explainable mystery.

In Ecclesiastes 11:5, Solomon marvels at one of the greatest mysteries of all time—the miracle of life. He draws the conclusion that our inability to explain the manner of development of a baby's bones from conception to childbirth is similar to our ignorance of the works of the Creator.

The context of this verse is similar to John 3:8, where Jesus explained to Nicodemus that the work of the Spirit to create new life is like wind blowing. Although the effects of wind can be seen, the wind itself cannot be seen.

Because we cannot see the conditions of people's hearts nor know who will accept God's love gift—Jesus—we are urged to sow seeds of truth in every way we can, at all times, to all people (see Ecclesiastes 11:6), knowing that salvation is God's work. We are to do our work and leave the results to God.

THE TAKEAWAY

One line from Dorothy Nolte's famous poem "Children Learn What They Live" is, *"If children live with acceptance, they learn to love."*

God's message to us is that He loves us dearly and accepts us just as we are. We don't have to clean ourselves up before we come to Him. We can come to Him right now with the assurance that He has already accepted us (see 1 John 4:19).

"We throw open our doors to God and discover at the same moment that he has already thrown open his door to us." (Romans 5:2 - MSG).

20

"Go, eat your bread with joy, and drink your wine with a merry heart, for God has already approved what you do. Let your garments be always white. Let not oil be lacking on your head." (Ecclesiastes 9:7-8 - ESV).

WHAT IS MEAL PLANNING?

- Meal planning is the process of building a weekly menu to best suit your nutritional needs. Some may be geared toward managing a specific health challenge, such as type 2 diabetes or heart disease.

- Some people follow a meal plan with a specific outcome in mind, such as weight loss or cholesterol improvement. An athlete may plan their meals to ensure they get enough nutrients for optimum performance.

- Others plan meals to stick to a food budget or map out meals for an entire family. People who aren't trying to manage a health challenge will typically make their own meal plans by selecting healthy recipes that their families enjoy.[9]

This study is about a very fascinating meal.

1. *What is the Lord's Supper?*

" ... the Lord Jesus on the same night in which He was betrayed took bread; and when He had given thanks, He broke it and said, "Take, eat; this is My body which is broken for you; do this in remembrance of Me." In the same manner He also took the cup

---

[9] https://www.everydayhealth.com/diet-nutrition/meal-planning/

after supper, saying, "This cup is the new covenant in My blood. This do, as often as you drink it, in remembrance of Me."" (1 Corinthians 11:23-25 - NKJV).

The Lord's Supper is a participation in the emblems of Jesus' body and blood as an expression of faith in Him. The emblems of Jesus' broken body and shed blood are symbolic of His death on behalf of sinners.

"But God commendeth his love toward us, in that, while we were yet sinners, Christ died for us." (Romans 5:8 - KJV).

2. *What did Jesus do before instituting the Lord's Supper?*

"[Jesus] rose from supper. He laid aside his outer garments, and taking a towel, tied it around his waist. Then he poured water into a basin and began to wash the disciples' feet and to wipe them with the towel that was wrapped around him." (John 13:4-5 - ESV).

Jesus and His disciples were about to celebrate the Passover meal together. Traditionally, a servant would wash the dust from the feet of weary travellers before the meal, but this time there was no servant to do this service. In an act of humility, Jesus stooped to perform this task Himself. The act of foot washing was symbolic of Jesus washing the disciples clean of sin (see John 13:10).

3. *What was the purpose of Jesus' example of washing His disciples' feet?*

"If I then, your Lord and Teacher, have washed your feet, you also ought to wash one another's feet. For I have given you an example, that you also should do just as I have done to you." (John 13:14-15 - ESV).

Jesus expects His followers to follow His example, humble themselves, and serve each other. This is the true expression of greatness in the kingdom of God.

4. *What is the purpose of the Lord's Supper?*

"For as often as ye eat this bread, and drink this cup, ye do shew the Lord's death till he come." (1 Corinthians 11:26 - KJV).

Christ instituted the Last Supper to be celebrated as a memorial of His great love for us. Taking communion symbolizes taking Jesus—body and blood—into ourselves. Just as God gave us access to His whole self through His sacrifice, we must choose to allow Him access to every part of our lives. Perfect love is giving one's whole self to others.

5. *What promise did Jesus make to His disciples about the Last Supper?*

"But I say unto you, I will not drink henceforth of this fruit of the vine, until that day when I drink it new with you in my Father's kingdom." (Matthew 26:29 - KJV).

When Christ instituted the Last Supper, He promised His disciples that He would not drink this wine again until He was reunited with His followers in His Father's kingdom. Partaking in the Lord's Supper also means celebrating the promise that Jesus is coming again to give us a seat at the banqueting table for a grand celebration dinner with His followers.

6. Is there an improper way to partake of the Lord's Supper?

"Wherefore whosoever shall eat this bread, and drink this cup of the Lord, unworthily, shall be guilty of the body and blood of the Lord." (1 Corinthians 11:27 - KJV).

Partaking of the symbolic bread and wine unworthily means doing so in the wrong spirit, without a heart open to internalise the benefits which flow from the death and sacrifice of Christ, such as the gifts of grace and freedom from sin. Self-examination is therefore required—reflecting upon the motives of the heart—before eating the bread or drinking from the cup (see 1 Corinthians 11:28) lest the communicant cuts himself off from the remedy for sin that our Lord and Saviour provided (see 1 Corinthians 11:29).

THE LESSON

Ecclesiastes 9:7 speaks of a man who receives the approval of God; God takes pleasure in his work. As a result, he is able to eat his bread and drink his wine—to enjoy his meal—with a merry heart. This is symbolic of contentment and freedom from condemnation. He is instructed in verse 8 to ensure that his garment is white (washed from all sin) and that the oil of gladness (see Isaiah 61:3) is not lacking from his head. In Roman culture, a white garment was worn by the guests at a festive banquet. Oil was poured generously on the heads of guests at feasts for their refreshment (see Psalm 23:5). It was a sign of divine favour (see Psalm 45:7). Lack of oil was a sign of mourning (see Matthew 6:17).

Jesus is so pleased with those who do the things that He commands, like loving and serving one another (see John 15:12,17), that He calls them His friends (see John 15:14). The interesting thing about serving is that those who serve are given a special position as friends. One privilege friends get is knowledge of what the Father's future plans are (see John 15:15). Another is receiving answers to their prayers (see John 15:16).

THE TAKEAWAY

The promise of Jesus' second coming was as tangible to the disciples as the many meals they shared together. If we want to sit at the great supper in the eternal kingdom and wear a white robe of righteousness, which has been washed clean by the blood of the Lamb (see Revelation 7:14), we have to learn to live in love and harmony with each other now. Certainly, that's the best meal planning that you can ever do!

DO GOOD ...

"I know that nothing is better for them than to rejoice, and to do good in their lives." (Ecclesiastes 3:12 - NKJV).

Work Ethics 1 - Diligence

"Whatever you find to do, do it well because where you are going—the grave—there will be no working or thinking or knowing or wisdom." (Ecclesiastes 9:10 – The Voice).

DID YOU KNOW?

- When buying lettuce seeds, there is a huge array of varieties to choose from, both tasty and decorative–from crisp and crunchy to succulent and juicy, vibrant green to deep red, frilly or smooth, and much more. One of the joys of growing your own is the wide diversity of leaves, far greater than you can buy in supermarkets. You can choose from various "hearting" types or fast-growing, loose-leafed, and salad-leaf mixes too.[10]

- Hearting lettuces, with their dense centre, generally take up to three months to reach harvesting size, and you cut the whole head when reaping. These are best grown in the ground, as they take up more space, but can also work in large containers. An example of this type is the iceberg lettuce.[11]

- Loose-leaf lettuces and salad-leaf mixes produce less dense rosettes of foliage, ideal for picking individual leaves and for growing in small spaces and containers. They can be highly decorative, both in the garden and on the plate, with a range of leaf colours, shapes, textures, and flavours. These are quicker to grow than hearting types, and you can often

---

[10] "How To Grow Lettuce", https://www.rhs.org.uk/vegetables/lettuce/grow-your-own
[11] Ibid

28

pick your first leaves only a month after sowing and continue for several weeks on a cut-and-come-again basis.[12]

BUDDING GARDENER

About a year after we moved house out of the capital city to a semi-rural parish, I bought a packet of lettuce seeds, which I planned to sow. Up to that time, I had no idea that there were so many varieties of lettuce! I also had to do some research on the ideal conditions for them to grow well.

In this study, we will explore the topic "spiritual gifts and ministries," which I believe are a lot like lettuce!

1. *Where do we get spiritual gifts from?*

"Each one of us has received a special gift in proportion to what Christ has given. As the scripture says, "When he went up to the very heights, he took many captives with him; he gave gifts to people." (Ephesians 4:7-8 - GNB).

Every believer born into the kingdom of God (see John 3:5) is given spiritual gifts (see 1 Peter 4:10).

2. *What are the different types of spiritual gifts?*

"There are diversities of gifts, but the same Spirit. There are differences of ministries, but the same Lord. ... there are diversities of activities, but it is the same God who works all in all." (1 Corinthians 12:4-6 - NKJV).

---

[12] Ibid

The best summary of the categories of spiritual gifts that I have seen came from a FAST Missions' course titled "Spiritual Gifts." Spiritual gifts may be classified as:

1. charisma or "personality gifts."
2. gifts of administration or "position gifts."
3. gifts of operation or "power gifts."[13]

3. What is the purpose of spiritual gifts?

"And He Himself gave some to be apostles, some prophets, some evangelists, and some pastors and teachers, for the equipping of the saints for the work of ministry, for the edifying of the body of Christ, till we all come to the unity of the faith and of the knowledge of the Son of God, to a perfect man, to the measure of the stature of the fullness of Christ." (Ephesians 4:11-13 - NKJV).

Spiritual gifts are given to believers to help them grow spiritually as individuals, to build up the body of Christ, and to work for the salvation of humanity. We are privileged to have these gifts for use in ministry.

4. What is the purpose of personality gifts?

"Having then gifts differing according to the grace that is given to us, let us use them: if prophecy, let us prophesy in proportion to our faith;" (Romans 12:6 - NKJV).

Personality gifts are given to every believer to help establish his or her special purpose in this world. They make us unique (see 1 Corinthians 12:19-20). These gifts create the inner drive that motivates ministry.

---

[13] "Spiritual Gifts", FAST Missions course

5. *What is the purpose of position gifts?*

"I therefore, the prisoner of the Lord, beseech you that ye walk worthy of the vocation wherewith ye are called." (Ephesians 4:1 - KJV).

Gifts of administration or position refer to any office or position, and also to specific ministries or tasks believers undertake. Examples of persons who have this gift include apostles, prophets, evangelists, pastors, and teachers (see Ephesians 4:11). These gifts are given for the work of the ministry, to build up the body of Christ (see Ephesians 4:12). They provide a solid structure that helps us to serve within the church.

6. *What is the purpose of power gifts?*

"And there are [distinctive] ways of working [to accomplish things], but it is the same God who produces all things in all believers [inspiring, energizing, and empowering them]." (1 Corinthians 12:6 - AMP).

"Power gifts, translated as "operations" of the Holy Spirit (see 1 Corinthians 12:6), describe special manifestations of the Holy Spirit."[14] Examples include the word of knowledge, faith, healing, and prophecy (see 1 Corinthians 12:8-10). These appear to be spontaneous gifts given by God to meet ministry needs of the moment.

7. *What is the ultimate purpose of spiritual gifts?*

"So we, being many, are one body in Christ, and every one members one of another." (Romans 12:5 - KJV).

---

[14] Ibid

We are given these gifts for ministry in the body of Christ. While they are different, the personality and position gifts must work together. We are promised that when we show up to work for God, the Holy Spirit will supply all the spiritual power we need to do His work (see Philippians 4:19).

THE LESSON

In Ecclesiastes 9, Solomon recognised the need for hard work in this context: we only get one earthly life to live. No work can be done when we die and are placed in the grave. The time to do work is now (see Ecclesiastes 3:22).

Structure and organisation are essential to church growth. This may look like gifted persons fitting into an existing frame to reach the needs of people in the community in which the church is situated. One such example is the deployment of deacons to minister to the needs of the poor in the early church (see Acts 6).

It could also look like a new structure being put in place to support the developing ministry of individuals. An example of this is establishing a discipleship group to nurture persons doing Bible study and joining the body of Christ while they are in prison.

THE TAKEAWAY

The key to maximising your potential is to know your core area of giftedness and to work in it. Living life with divine purpose, on purpose, will make your ministry blossom and grow, and your life will be more fulfilling. Make this your daily motto: *"Whatever your hand finds to do, do it wholeheartedly, serving as to the Lord and not unto men."* Do whatever it takes to set people free from the prison house of sin.

Work Ethics 2 - Faith

"Cast your bread upon the waters, For you will find it after many days." (Ecclesiastes 11:1 - NKJV).

DID YOU KNOW?

- Angel hair noodles, or capellini, are a staple in many kitchens worldwide. Their delicate, thin strands make them unique among pasta types, offering a light and versatile option for various dishes.

- *History and Origin:* Angel hair pasta traces its roots back to Italy, where it has been enjoyed for centuries. Known as "capellini" in Italian, which means "little hairs," this pasta is one of the thinnest types available.

- *Cooking time:* Because the strands are so thin, they cook rapidly, typically in two to four minutes. This makes it an excellent choice for quick meals.

- *Pairing with Sauces:* Due to its delicate nature, angel hair pasta is best suited for lighter sauces. Olive oil, garlic, and fresh herbs are all you need to create a delicious meal![15]

Throughout the Bible, we can see an interesting interplay: the interaction between humanity and angels. That is our topic for this study.

---

[15] "What You Need To Know About Angel Hair Pasta"
https://eatnaturalheaven.com/blogs/blog/what-you-need-to-know-about-angel-hair-pasta#:~:text

1. *What is the role of angels according to Psalm 103:20-21, Psalm 104:4, and Hebrews 1:14?*

"Bless the LORD, you His angels, who excel in strength, who do His word, heeding the voice of His word. Bless the LORD, all you His hosts, you ministers of His, who do His pleasure." (Psalm 103:20-21 - NKJV).

"The angels are his messengers—his servants of fire!" (Psalm 104:4 - TLB).

"Are they not all ministering spirits sent forth to minister for those who will inherit salvation?" (Hebrews 1:14 - NKJV).

Angels or messengers are God's ministers. They stand ready to do God's will on behalf of fallen humanity.

All throughout Scripture, we see that God sent angels with important messages to humanity.

2. *What was the role of angels in ministering to Lot in Genesis 19:1,12-13?*

"Now the two angels came to Sodom in the evening, and Lot was sitting in the gate of Sodom. When Lot saw them, he rose to meet them, and he bowed himself with his face toward the ground. Then the men said to Lot, "Have you anyone else here? Son-in-law, your sons, your daughters, and whomever you have in the city—take them out of this place! For we will destroy this place, because the outcry against them has grown great before the face of the LORD, and the LORD has sent us to destroy it." (Genesis 19:1,12-13 - NKJV).

Angels were sent to warn Lot and his family of the impending destruction of Sodom. Lot heeded their counsel to leave the city, and his life was saved. Before leaving, he tried to influence his sons-in-law to follow him (see Genesis 19:14), but he was unsuccessful. They refused to leave and died in the city when it was destroyed.

3. *What was the role of angels in ministering to Jacob in Genesis 28:12?*

"Then he dreamed, and behold, a ladder was set up on the earth, and its top reached to heaven; and there the angels of God were ascending and descending on it." (Genesis 28:12 - NKJV).

Jacob was a fugitive on the run from his brother, Esau, after he stole his blessing. On his way from Beer-sheba to Haran, he paused to rest at Beth-el, and there he had a dream. In his dream, he saw a ladder reaching from earth to heaven with angels going up and down on it. Christ is the ladder that Jacob saw (see John 1:51). Angels relay messages between earth and heaven—such as the interpretation of dreams and visions. They take prayers to the Father and bring answers to prayers (see Daniel 8:16 and Luke 1:13).

4. *What was the role of angels in ministering to Jesus in the wilderness?*

"Then the devil left Him, and behold, angels came and ministered to Him." (Matthew 4:11 - NKJV).

Jesus commenced His Galilean ministry with 40 days of fasting. Afterward, He was tempted by Satan to forgo His mission to redeem humanity (see Matthew 4:1-10). Jesus warded off each temptation that Satan threw at Him with the Word of God. Frustrated with Jesus' refusal to presume upon His Father's power and protection, Satan left Him for a season (see Luke 4:13). Ministering angels came to strengthen Jesus with food and to comfort Him after His victory over Satan.

5. How are the followers of Christ like ministering angels?

"Ye are the light of the world. A city that is set on an hill cannot be hid. Let your light so shine before men, that they may see your good works, and glorify your Father which is in heaven." *(Matthew 5:14,16 - KJV).*

Those who are consecrated to God will become channels of light and blessing. God will make them His agents to communicate the riches of His grace to others (see Ezekiel 34:26).

6. How can we maximise our impact for the kingdom of God?

"Neither do men light a candle, and put it under a bushel, but on a candlestick; and it giveth light unto all that are in the house." *(Matthew 5:15 - KJV).*

The Greek word for "bushel" is used in the New Testament to describe a covering that conceals light. Followers of Christ are counselled against doing anything that might conceal the light.

If we wish to direct others in the path of righteousness, we must live out the principles of righteousness in our lives. This will be seen in holy conversations, unswerving integrity, acts of kindness such as giving bread to the needy and living a consistent, godly life.

THE LESSON

The Preacher admonishes us in Ecclesiastes 11:1 to cast our bread upon the waters and to claim the promise that we will find it after many days; not immediately, but in due time and when it is least expected. First, we should pray for direction to know whom to share the bread of life with, then launch out in faith and share the message of salvation with people God wants to save, not worrying about if and when they will accept the invitation to answer God's call. We are called to share our faith in Jesus (see Matthew 5:14-16). Salvation is God's part.

Whenever we step out in faith to minister for God and are engaged in His service, we are guaranteed that Satan will seek to take us off our course. Temptations will assail us, and we will face challenges. It is then that we must remember the promises that all who will live godly in Christ Jesus shall suffer persecution (see 2 Timothy 3:12); that if we look to God, we will receive grace to resist and overcome any temptation (see 1 Corinthians 10:13). We can rejoice in tribulations, knowing that in trials and challenges we learn patience, we gain experience, and our hope is confirmed (see Romans 5:1-5).

THE TAKEAWAY

When we work with God to minister to perishing souls, we are promised the companionship of angels. Thousands upon thousands and ten thousand times ten thousand angels are waiting to cooperate with us to communicate the light of truth that God has generously given, that His people may be prepared for the coming of Christ.

Work Ethics 3: Hope

"He who observes the wind will not sow, and he who regards the clouds will not reap." (Ecclesiastes 11:4 - NKJV).

DID YOU KNOW?

Honey's ability to stay fresh for thousands of years is due to its unique chemical composition. Let's break it down:

- *Low Water Content*: Honey is hygroscopic, meaning it contains very little water. Most bacteria and microorganisms need water to grow and survive. With a water content of less than 18%, honey provides an inhospitable environment for these tiny invaders.

- *High Acidity*: Honey has a pH level between 3.2 and 4.5, making it acidic. This high acidity level prevents the growth of bacteria and other microorganisms that could spoil the honey.

- *Hydrogen Peroxide*: Bees add an enzyme called glucose oxidase to honey, which produces small amounts of hydrogen peroxide. This acts as a natural preservative, further protecting honey from spoilage.[16]

I was recently introduced to honey made by bees that were fed a diet of mangoes and blackcurrant/jamun/java plum/ribena fruits. The astonishing result? Richer, darker, sweeter-tasting honey!

---

[16] "The Sweet Science of Honey: Exploring an Ancient Wonder Through STEM", June 12, 2024 https://stemfinity.com/blogs/stem-facts/the-sweet-science-of-honey-exploring-an-ancient-wonder-through-stem#:~:text=

This study examines the spiritual gift of prophecy.

1. What is one purpose of Bible prophecy?

"Now I tell you before it comes, that when it does come to pass, you may believe that I am He." (John 13:19 - NKJV).

The primary subject of Bible prophecy is Christ. In the Old Testament, He is symbolised in the sacrificial service, portrayed in the law, and revealed by the prophets. In the New Testament, numerous prophecies fulfilled in the life and ministry of Jesus let us know that He is the Messiah. Prophecy is designed to enhance our relationship with God.

- *Prophecies of Christ's sufferings and death*

" But I am a worm, and no man; A reproach of men, and despised by the people. All those who see Me ridicule Me; They shoot out the lip, they shake the head, saying, "He trusted in the Lord, let Him rescue Him; Let Him deliver Him, since He delights in Him!"" (Psalm 22:6-8 - NKJV).

"He is despised and rejected by men, a Man of sorrows and acquainted with grief. And we hid, as it were, our faces from Him; He was despised, and we did not esteem Him." (Isaiah 53:3 - NKJV).

- *Fulfilment: Jesus is mocked on the cross*

And those who passed by blasphemed Him, wagging their heads. He trusted in God; let Him deliver Him now if He will have Him; for He said, 'I am the Son of God.'" (Matthew 27:39,43 - NKJV).

Through the psalmist, Christ had foretold the treatment that He would receive from men. Isaiah's prophecies of Christ's sufferings and death were unmistakably plain.

2.   What is another purpose of Bible prophecy?

"And now I have told you before it comes, that when it does come to pass, you may believe." (John 14:29 - NKJV).

Fulfilled Bible prophecies confirm that God and the Scriptures can be trusted.

- *Prophecy of last day events: Signs in nature*

"The sun shall be turned into darkness, and the moon into blood, Before the coming of the great and awesome day of the Lord." (Joel 2:31 - NKJV).

- *Fulfilment in history: The Dark Day (May 19, 1780)*

May 19, 1780 stands in history as "The Dark Day." On this day in history, a strange darkness fell over much of New England. It was so dark by noon that it was impossible to read or write, even while sitting by a window. The darkness that enveloped Connecticut remained there for a day and a half.[17]

The description of this event, as given by eyewitnesses, is an echo of the words of the Lord, recorded by the prophet Joel 2500 years prior to their fulfilment.

---

[17] "Dark Day – Today in History: May 19", https://connecticuthistory.org/dark-day-today-in-history-may-19/#:~:text=

3. *What does prophecy provide to those who understand it?*

"For whatever things were written before were written for our learning, that we through the patience and comfort of the Scriptures might have hope." (Romans 15:4 - NKJV).

Bible prophecies provide hope for the people of God. We are reassured by many fulfilled prophecies that future events prophesied in Scripture, such as the second coming of Christ, will also come to pass.

- *Prophecy: The Lord will pour out His Spirit in the last days*

"And it shall come to pass afterward that I will pour out My Spirit on all flesh; Your sons and your daughters shall prophesy, Your old men shall dream dreams, Your young men shall see visions. And also on My menservants and on My maidservants I will pour out My Spirit in those days." (Joel 2:28-29 – NKJV).

- *Fulfilment: The Day of Pentecost (see Acts 2:1-11)*

On the Day of Pentecost, the disciples were filled with the Holy Ghost, which enabled them to speak fluently in languages (tongues) that they had not known before.

4. *What is the result of having the gift of prophecy in the body of Christ?*

"Now the God of patience and consolation grant you to be likeminded one toward another according to Christ Jesus: That ye may with one mind and one mouth glorify God, even the Father of our Lord Jesus Christ." (Romans 15:5-6 - KJV).

The gift of prophecy is given to believers to foster the spirit of unity in the body of Christ (see Ephesians 4:3). Unity among believers brings glory and honour to God.

5. *How has the gift of prophecy been seen among the remnant?*

- *Prophecy: God's Spirit poured out among the remnant*

"And it shall come to pass that whoever calls on the name of the Lord shall be saved. For in Mount Zion and in Jerusalem there shall be deliverance, as the Lord has said, among the remnant whom the Lord calls." (Joel 2:32 - NKJV).

- *Fulfilment: The Gift of Prophecy in the ministry of Ellen G. White*

The prophetic gift was manifested in the ministry of Ellen G. White. She is the most translated American non-fiction author and made a significant contribution to the health reform movement in nineteenth-century America. By the time she passed away, her writings came close to 100,000 pages. This included 24 published books, 5,000 articles, and more than 200 informational leaflets.[18] Her prolific writings offer comfort, guidance, instruction, and correction to the body of Christ.

6. *What prophecy is given concerning the remnant in the last days?*

"And the dragon was enraged with the woman, and he went to make war with the rest of her offspring, who keep the commandments of God and have the testimony of Jesus Christ." (Revelation 12:17 - NKJV).

---

[18] "Who Was Ellen G. White?", https://www.adventist.org/who-was-ellen-g-white/

God's remnant people will face great trial and distress. Those who keep the commandments of God and the faith of Jesus will feel the anger of the dragon and his hosts. It is prophesied that a faithful group of people will resist Satan's dominion and will stand for Christ (see Revelation 12:11-12 and Daniel 12:1).

THE LESSON

In Ecclesiastes 11:4, the Preacher warns that those who look for difficulty in every situation will never initiate any new project. If we wait for all obstacles to be removed from our pathway and demand certainty of success before acting, we may never take the first step on a journey and may never get any work done.

THE TAKEAWAY

Look for opportunities as you work in spite of obvious challenges. Remember that God knows the end from the beginning, and just like honey, He has preserved His Word over millennia that we may know He will be with us throughout our lives (see 2 Corinthians 1:22). Finally, when we recognise that all the promises of God are fulfilled in Christ Jesus (see 2 Corinthians 1:20), we can hang our hope on the sure promise of a future life through Him.

Love Conquers All

"Woe to thee, O land, when thy king is a child, and thy princes eat in the morning! Blessed art thou, O land, when thy king is the son of nobles, and thy princes eat in due season, for strength, and not for drunkenness!" (Ecclesiastes 10:16-17 - KJV).

DID YOU KNOW?

- Breakfast is often called "the most important meal of the day," and for good reason.

- As the name suggests, breakfast breaks the overnight fasting period. It replenishes your supply of glucose to boost your energy levels and alertness while also providing other essential nutrients required for good health.

- Many studies have shown the health benefits of eating breakfast. It improves your energy levels and ability to concentrate in the short term, and can help with better weight management, and reduce the risk of type 2 diabetes and heart disease in the long term.[19]

The focus of this study is the Law of God.

1. How is the Law described in Romans 7:12?

"Wherefore the law is holy, and the commandment holy, and just, and good." (Romans 7:12 - KJV).

---

[19] "Breakfast", https://www.betterhealth.vic.gov.au/health/healthyliving/breakfast

44

The Law is a revelation of the character of its Author. As God is holy, so the Law of God is holy, just, and good. As God is unchanging (see Malachi 3:6), so His Law is unchanging.

2. *Where can we find the Law?*

"For the same one who said, "Do not commit adultery," also said, "Do not commit murder." Even if you do not commit adultery, you have become a lawbreaker if you commit murder." (James 2:11 - GNT).

The Ten Commandments (see Exodus 20:1-17 and Deuteronomy 5:6-21) were given to Moses by God at Mount Sinai and are referred to as the Law.

3. *What is the main principle of the Law?*

"Jesus said unto him, Thou shalt love the Lord thy God with all thy heart, and with all thy soul, and with all thy mind. This is the first and great commandment. And the second is like unto it, Thou shalt love thy neighbour as thyself. On these two commandments hang all the law and the prophets." (Matthew 22:37-40 - KJV).

Love is the foundational principle of God's Law. Both of these commandments are an expression of the principle of love; love for God and love for man.

4. *What is the purpose of the Ten Commandments?*

"Everyone who sins breaks the law; in fact, sin is lawlessness." (1 John 3:4 – NIV).

The Ten Commandments were given to point out sin and to lead us to the law of love. Without this law, humanity has no clear idea of the purity and holiness of God's character nor of their own guilt or uncleanness. Seeing our true state in the mirror of the perfect law of liberty (see Psalm 19:7 and James 1:23, 25) helps us to come to God for cleansing.

5. *What lesson did Jesus teach in John 14:15?*

"If you love me, keep My commandments." (John 14:15 - NKJV).

Jesus taught that true love for God will be shown by obedience to all His commandments (see 1 John 5:3).

6. *Where does God want His law?*

"This is the covenant that I will make with them after those days, saith the Lord, I will put my laws into their hearts, and in their minds will I write them." (Hebrews 10:16 - KJV).

God wants to place His law of love in our minds and write His principles of benevolence in our hearts.

7. *What blessing is promised to God's faithful commandment keepers? (see Revelation 22:14).*

Great rewards are promised to those who keep God's commandments faithfully (see Psalm 19:11). Those who have the principle of love written in their hearts will be granted access to the tree of life in the paradise of God (see Revelation 2:7). This blessing was lost when Adam and Eve disobeyed God's law of love in Eden.

THE LESSON

In the tradition of the Preacher's day, consultations dealing with government matters and administering justice took place in the mornings (see Jeremiah 21:12). Morning was the time for religion and having devotion.

- *Cursed*

A curse was pronounced upon the land in Ecclesiastes 10:16 because the rulers were children. The word "children" was not a reference to the age of the rulers.

When the Preacher said a child was king, he was referring to an immature, inexperienced ruler who did not manage his responsibilities well and ate in the mornings. Of course, nothing was wrong with eating breakfast! Earlier, I highlighted many good reasons why breakfast is considered the most important meal.

The challenge with the young, immature ruler was this: he ate bread *before* offering the morning sacrifice. His priorities were wrong. To compound the situation, his advisors, ministers of state, and counsellors—all who were supposed to provide guidance—were also neglecting their duty; leaving the young ruler to figure things out for himself while they indulged in feasting and banqueting.

- *Blessed*

A blessing was pronounced on the land in Ecclesiastes 10:17 because the king was the son of royalty. The princes ate in season; for strength and not for drunkenness. This ruler did not have an unfair advantage by virtue of his noble birth, but his noble virtues set him apart.

The distinction between the childish ruler and his advisors, and the noble's son and those he ruled, can be seen in how they treated food. The nobles did not eat until duty was attended to, recognising that there is a right time for everything (see Ecclesiastes 3:1). They ate to refresh the body and to be strengthened to do the king's business, not merely to satisfy their taste buds nor indulge themselves in sensual pleasures.

The members of the government of God also operate on the principle of putting first things first. They govern a kingdom built upon the foundation of the law of love. This magnificent, other-centred love manifests itself in the way its members treat each other. They all elevate each other above self, putting each other first and giving of themselves sacrificially for the benefit of their subjects.

THE TAKEAWAY

We too must live lives built on this foundation of love—giving ourselves to God first, in the morning of our lives (see Ecclesiastes 12:1), so that He can give us new hearts with the capacity to really love others; to want what is best for them and to exercise our power to help them. I think you would agree that there is no better way to start each day!

A Sweet Treat

"The sleep of a labouring man is sweet, whether he eat little or much: but the abundance of the rich will not suffer him to sleep."
(Ecclesiastes 5:12 - KJV).

Have you ever wondered about the difference between sponge cakes and butter cakes? Both are similar at a glance but look deeper, and you will see these two confections couldn't be more different.

- Sponge cakes are light and fluffy, getting their name from the slightly spongy texture that won't hold up to a heavy frosting. Butter cakes are heavier and more dense, with a hearty weight to each bite. Butter cakes can be exceptionally moist and do well with many kinds of frostings and glazes.

- The light texture of sponge cakes is due to air that's mixed into the batter. In order to make a sponge cake, you really only need three ingredients—sugar, flour, and eggs—which makes for a relatively simple-to-fix cake. Some cooks take out the yolks and use just the egg whites, which will create a lighter but drier cake.

- Butter cakes range from pound cakes to red velvet to classic yellow cake with chocolate frosting. While each variant of butter cake has its own recipe, all share two common factors—they include butter or oil and also a leavening agent like baking powder.[20]

---

[20] "Butter vs. Sponge Cake: What's the Difference?", September 19, 2023, https://www.yahoo.com/lifestyle/butter-vs-sponge-cake-whats-111500046.html

CHILDHOOD MEMORIES

My childhood memories include watching my mom bake the traditional Guyana black cake. The recipe for this fruit cake included preserved fruits, burnt sugar, butter, eggs, flour, and select spices. Preparation and baking time usually lasted about three hours.

This was a sweet treat we children would look forward to at Christmas. Our family's Christmas tradition included going over to our neighbours to share cake, sweets, and nuts. After a while, this type of cake became more popular, and we would get it more often than once a year, at times even helping Mom mix it!

In this study, we will look at an extra-special sweet treat that God has provided for all of His creation.

> *1. According to Genesis 2:1-3 and Exodus 20:9-10, which day is the Sabbath of the Lord?*

"Thus the heavens and the earth, and all the host of them, were finished. And on the seventh day God ended His work which He had done, and He rested on the seventh day from all His work which He had done. Then God blessed the seventh day and sanctified it, because in it He rested from all His work which God had created and made." (Genesis 2:1-3 - NKJV).

"Six days you shall labor and do all your work, but the seventh day is the Sabbath of the Lord your God ..." (Exodus 20:9-10a - NKJV).

The seventh day of the week is the Sabbath day. In lesson 6, we concluded that each day of creation week was a literal 24-hour day. The Sabbath is a weekly tradition that was designed by God at the end of the creation week for the benefit of all humanity (see Mark 2:27).

2. *How can we be certain which day is the seventh day?*

"Now when the Sabbath was past, Mary Magdalene, Mary the mother of James, and Salome bought spices, that they might ... anoint Him. Very early in the morning, on the first day of the week, they came to the tomb when the sun had risen." (Mark 16:1-2 - NKJV).

This is Mark's account of Jesus' death and resurrection. Prophecy predicts, and history confirms, that Jesus died on Friday afternoon, rested in the tomb on Saturday, and was resurrected early on Sunday morning. We can conclude from this that Sunday is the first day of the week. It therefore means that the seventh day is Saturday.

3. *What time does the Sabbath begin and end?*

"It shall be to you a sabbath of solemn rest ... from evening to evening, you shall celebrate your sabbath." (Leviticus 23:32 - NKJV).

According to the Bible, each day begins at sunset and ends the next sunset. The dark part of the day comes first (see Genesis 1:5, 8, 13, 19, 23, 31). The Sabbath begins at sunset on Friday and ends at sunset on Saturday.

4. *What are the three main purposes of the Sabbath?*

"Six days shall work be done, but the seventh day is a Sabbath of solemn rest, a holy convocation. You shall do no work on it; it is the Sabbath of the Lord in all your dwellings." (Leviticus 23:3 - NKJV).

- Rest

The Sabbath was established as a time for rest from regular work, for physical restoration for a man and all of his household (see Exodus 20:8-11).

- Relationship

It was also set aside as a special time for communing with God and His people (see Leviticus 23:3).

- Restoration

The Sabbath is also a day for ministering to people in need (see Matthew 12:12). Jesus spent much time teaching, healing, and restoring people to wholeness on the Sabbath.

   5. Which day is the Lord's Day?

"If you turn away your foot from the Sabbath, from doing your pleasure on My holy day ..." (Isaiah 58:13 - NKJV).

The Bible speaks of the Lord's day in Revelation 1:10, so it is clear that the Lord does have a special day. Isaiah 58:13 identifies the Sabbath as the Lord's day. The Sabbath is the only day that was blessed by the Lord and claimed by Him as His holy day. The Sabbath is the Lord's day, as Jesus is the Lord of the Sabbath (see Mark 2:28).

   6. How can we honour God on the Sabbath day?

""If you keep your feet from breaking the Sabbath and from doing as you please on my holy day, if you call the Sabbath a delight and the Lord's holy day honorable, and if you honor it by

not going your own way and not doing as you please or speaking idle words, then you will find your joy in the Lord, and I will cause you to ride in triumph on the heights of the land and to feast on the inheritance of your father Jacob." For the mouth of the Lord has spoken." (Isaiah 58:13-14 – NIV).

God is honoured when we take time out from doing our own business, seeking our own pleasure, and speaking unholy words on the Sabbath, and choosing to spend quality time with Him. In practice, this means not going to work, not partaking in entertainment, and not having conversations about everyday, commonplace things.

> 7. *What special blessing is promised to those who keep the Sabbath holy?*

"I ... gave them My Sabbaths, to be a sign between them and Me, that they might know that I am the LORD who sanctifies them." (Ezekiel 20:12 - NKJV).

The assurance is given that those who keep the Sabbath holy will be sanctified by God. They will receive joy and peace that fills the soul like a sweet song that never ends.

THE LESSON

The Preacher reminds us in Ecclesiastes 5:12 that the sleep of a labouring or a working man is sweet, whether he eats little or eats much. In direct contrast, the abundance of the rich man will not allow him to sleep peacefully.

The man who spends his time and energy on work, including working for God, enjoys sweet sleep even if he eats a little because he is not burdened with the cares and fears of the rich. If he eats much, because of his healthy lifestyle, he does not suffer indigestion, which often disturbs the sleep of the indulgent, rich man.

The Sabbath is an oasis in time for God to have sweet fellowship with humanity. It is an opportunity for us to get to know God as much as He knows us and to know that He loves us as we are. It is a weekly reminder that, as created beings, we are dependent upon our Creator for life and provisions. When we rest, we show that we accept His love and care for us, and we trust Him to restore His image in us.

THE TAKEAWAY

Make Sabbath-keeping a part of your family tradition. Keep the seventh day holy now so that you can live in the land flowing with milk and honey (see Deuteronomy 6:3 and Ezekiel 20:6), where the Sabbath will be kept weekly throughout the ceaseless ages of eternity (see Isaiah 66:23). What a sweet day that will be!

Soul Food

"Behold that which I have seen: it is good and comely for one to eat and to drink, and to enjoy the good of all his labour that he taketh under the sun all the days of his life, which God giveth him: for it is his portion. Every man also to whom God hath given riches and wealth, and hath given him power to eat thereof, and to take his portion, and to rejoice in his labour; this is the gift of God." (Ecclesiastes 5:18-19 - KJV).

The kitchen is often referred to as the heart of the home, and for good reason. It is where we prepare food, gather with family and friends, and create memories that last a lifetime. Over the years, many kitchen devices have been invented to help us save time, energy, and money.

DID YOU KNOW?

- The first refrigerator was invented by Jacob Perkins in 1834. It used ether vapor compression to cool the air, but it wasn't until the early 1900s that electric refrigerators became popular.

- The first modern dishwasher was invented by Josephine Cochrane in 1886. She wanted a machine that could wash dishes faster and more efficiently than her servants.

- The microwave was invented by accident in 1945 by Percy Spencer, an engineer at Raytheon. While working on a radar system, he noticed that a candy bar in his pocket had melted. Intrigued, he experimented with different foods and discovered that microwaves could be used to cook food quickly.[21]

My brother gave my husband and me money to buy a microwave as a wedding gift when we got married in 2007. We decided not to get one and bought an extra mattress instead. Over the years, we've used it to host over a dozen guests in our home. Those times have really been a blessing to us.

This study is about stewardship.

1. Who is the source of all that we have?

"Both riches and honor come from You, and You reign over all. In Your hand is power and might; In Your hand it is to make great and to give strength to all." (1 Chronicles 29:12 - NKJV).

We get life from our loving Creator. We also receive riches and strength from His generous hand. Without Him, we are nothing.

2. What is stewardship?

"And the LORD God took the man, and put him into the garden of Eden to dress it and to keep it." (Genesis 2:15 - KJV).

Stewardship is the privilege of managing the resources God entrusted to us. It is a response of thankfulness and praise to God for being who He is and for what He has done for us (see 1 Chronicles 29:13).

---

[21] "10 Fun Kitchen Facts For 2023", https://rachiele.com/dinos-blog/f/10-fun-kitchen-facts

3. What is one form of stewardship?

"Bring ye all the tithes into the storehouse, that there may be meat in mine house, and prove me now herewith, saith the LORD of hosts, if I will not open you the windows of heaven, and pour you out a blessing, that there shall not be room enough to receive it." *(Malachi 3:10 - KJV).*

According to Smith's Bible Dictionary, the *tithe* or tenth is the proportion of property devoted to religious uses. Two prominent instances of tithing are Abram presenting one-tenth of the spoils of his victory to Melchizedek (see Genesis 14:20 and Hebrews 7:2, 6) and Jacob, after his vision at Luz, devoting a tenth of all his property to God in case he should return home in safety (see Genesis 28:22). The first enactment of the law in respect of the tithe is found in Leviticus 27:30-33. The main purpose of the tithe was for the maintenance of the priests engaged in the service of the Lord (see 2 Chronicles 31:5-6,11-12).

4. What is another form of stewardship?

"For it hath pleased them of Macedonia and Achaia to make a certain contribution for the poor saints which are at Jerusalem." *(Romans 15:26 - KJV).*

Presenting freewill offerings and gifts to God in response to His generosity is also one form of stewardship (see examples in 1 Chronicles 29:14, 17 and 2 Chronicles 31:10, 14). These offerings are used to spread the gospel and help those in need. The habit of giving offerings helps us to love others and gain victory over selfishness and covetousness.

5. *What other forms of stewardship are there?*

"Therefore, I urge you, brothers and sisters, in view of God's mercy, to offer your bodies as a living sacrifice, holy and pleasing to God—this is your true and proper worship." (Romans 12:1 – NIV).

God wants us to give ourselves to Him. He wants us to submit every area of our lives to His control. In addition to property and possessions, we are also stewards of gifts of time, opportunities, and abilities.

6. *What is God's desire for stewards?*

"Moreover it is required in stewards, that a man be found faithful." (1 Corinthians 4:2 - KJV).

All who are stewards are called to be faithful—to recognise that what they have been given is not their own (see 1 Corinthians 6:19-20) and to make the best use of the resources in their care to further the business of the Lord. See 2 Chronicles 30:20-21 for an example of faithful stewardship in Hezekiah's life.

THE LESSON

Life is God's gift. The Preacher reminds us in Ecclesiastes 5:18-19 that the ability to truly enjoy the rewards of our labour and the pleasures that money can buy—such as good food and drink—is also a gift from God. This is an echo of Ecclesiastes 2:24, *"There is nothing better for a man, than that he should eat and drink, and that he should make his soul enjoy good in his labour. This also I saw, that it was from the hand of God" (KJV)*, and Ecclesiastes 3:13, *"And also that every man should eat and drink, and enjoy the good of all his labour, it is the gift of God." (KJV)*.

58

The manner in which Solomon refers to God as the Giver, both of life and its enjoyments, shows that they ought to be received and used consistently with His will, and for His glory. He concludes in Ecclesiastes 5:20 that having made a proper use of riches, a man will remember the days of his past life with pleasure.

THE TAKEAWAY

No matter how much or how little we have in life, we must remember that it is God alone who gives contentment (see 1 Timothy 6:6) and that the bigger blessing is in giving, not in receiving (see Acts 20:35).

Here's how Solomon puts it, *"I know that there is no good in them, but for a man to rejoice, and to do good in his life." (Ecclesiastes 3:12 – KJV).*

Recipe for Disaster

"And whatever my eyes desired I did not keep from them. I kept my heart from no pleasure, for my heart found pleasure in all my toil, and this was my reward for all my toil." (Ecclesiastes 2:10 - ESV).

DID YOU KNOW?

- When consumed in moderate quantities, coconut can help to keep you full between meals. This effect can reduce your overall food intake and promote weight loss.

- Excessive consumption of coconut can, however, lead to weight gain, as this food is high in fat and calories. In addition, when incorporated into other high-calorie recipes, such as puddings, cakes, and ice cream, for example, coconut can also lead to unintended weight gain.[22]

MY CULINARY MISHAP

My food and nutrition class in high school included a practical cooking component. This consisted of the preparation of specific dishes to align with the circumstances in a case study. My menu included a dessert called "coconut biscuits," which are very firm cookies made from shredded coconut flakes, sugar, and egg whites—the key ingredients needed to give these cookies their crunch.

Due to the time pressure of the moment, my batch of a dozen cookies was very badly burnt. That dish was almost a total disaster. Thankfully, I was able to salvage three cookies, which I gladly

---

[22] "7 Coconut Benefits for your Health (plus Nutrition and Recipes", https://www.tuasaude.com/en/coconut-benefits/#:~:text=

placed onto the display plate for inspection, garnished with strands of artificially coloured, shredded coconut.

The lesson I learnt was: *"If you have something big to do, practice beforehand if possible."* In my case, there was a detailed time plan of what-to-do when, but I had not practiced making all the dishes on the menu under the 3-hour time constraint while washing up the dishes.

This study examines Christian behaviour.

1. *What guiding principle should govern the lives of the people of God?*

"But you are a chosen generation, a royal priesthood, a holy nation, His own special people, that you may proclaim the praises of Him who called you out of darkness into His marvelous light." (1 Peter 2:9 - NKJV).

We are called to be godly people who think, feel, and act in harmony with the principles of heaven. In essence, while here on earth, we must live righteous lives that promote Christlike purity, health, and joy.

2. *How does being a Christian affect one's behaviour?*

"Therefore, I urge you, brothers and sisters, in view of God's mercy, to offer your bodies as a living sacrifice, holy and pleasing to God—this is your true and proper worship." (Romans 12:1 – NIV).

In light of the context of Romans 11:36, that is, that every living thing originates from God, all things continue to live and exist through Him, and all things are directed to Him, Romans 12:1

informs us that we have been given the privilege to worship God—to give Him glory and honour forever. This will impact our physical, emotional, and mental choices.

3. *What principle should guide the diet of God's called-out people?*

" ... whether you eat or drink, or whatever you do, do all to the glory of God." (1 Corinthians 10:31 - NKJV).

The link between diet and overall health is unmistakable. Over the years, studies have shown numerous benefits accruing to those who follow God's original whole-food, plant-based diet (see Genesis 1:29). A wholesome diet should exclude unclean foods (see Leviticus 11).

Any substance that has the potential to harm the body and the mind should be avoided completely. This includes alcohol, caffeine, tobacco, narcotics, dangerous drugs, and even some prescription drugs.

4. *What principle is provided to promote good mental health among God's called-out people?*

"Casting down arguments and every high thing that exalts itself against the knowledge of God, bringing every thought into captivity to the obedience of Christ." (2 Corinthians 10:5 - NKJV).

God wants us to have clear, healthy minds so He can communicate His message of love to us, and we can share this message with the people in our circle of influence whom He wants to save.

Good mental health care will include demolishing ideas, arguments, doctrines, teachings, or concepts that infect the mind and distort the truth about God as revealed by Jesus Christ (see 2 Corinthians 10:5).

5. *What other areas are important to maintaining a healthy lifestyle?*

"Beloved, I pray that you may prosper in all things and be in health, just as your soul prospers." (3 John 1:2 - NKJV).

Exercise: Exercise is an essential component for maintaining optimum health for people of every age. One of the most effective forms of exercise is brisk walking. The benefits of walking are further enhanced when done outdoors in the early morning sunlight and fresh air.

Rest: Rest is critical for recharging our physical, mental, emotional, and spiritual batteries. This includes getting adequate sleep for one's age and taking a weekly break from work to celebrate the Sabbath of the Creator (see Exodus 20:8-11).

6. *What principle should guide the dress of God's called-out people?*

"Your beauty should not come from outward adornment, such as elaborate hairstyles and the wearing of gold jewelry or fine clothes. Rather, it should be that of your inner self, the unfading beauty of a gentle and quiet spirit, which is of great worth in God's sight." (1 Peter 3:3-4 – NIV).

The dress choices of God's special people should reflect Godly standards. Clothing should be tasteful, well-fitting, appropriate for the occasion, modest (offering proper cover to the wearer), not given to outward show, and should reflect financial responsibility, avoiding extravagance.

7. *What principle should guide the recreational activity of God's called-out people?*

"Finally, brothers and sisters, whatever is true, whatever is noble, whatever is right, whatever is pure, whatever is lovely, whatever is admirable—if anything is excellent or praiseworthy—think about such things." (Philippians 4:8 – NIV).

The etymology of the words *amusement* and *entertainment* are very informative. A-muse-ment means "without a thought" or "without thinking." It's really putting one's self in a state of "mindless-ness." Enter-tain-ment is about what happens when something is allowed to *enter* a con*tain*er, such as the mind, and takes control of it. Christians should focus on recreational activities that elevate their thoughts and spend time in ways that please God, our Creator. This will impact our associations, the places we go to, the games we play, the literature we read, the things we look at, how we spend our screen time, and our music choices. Worldly amusement and entertainment should be avoided (see 1 John 2:15-17).

THE LESSON

Despite having everything that his eyes desired—wine, houses, food, livestock, riches, and worldly entertainment (see Ecclesiastes 2:1-10)—the pleasure Solomon gained was only temporary (see Ecclesiastes 2:11).

The good news of Jesus Christ is more than facts to be believed by faith; it is also a life to be lived—a life of righteousness befitting a follower of Jesus Christ.

Practice for living eternally starts now. The spiritual warm-up for the journey includes walking in love—caring for the interests of others as well as ourselves (see Philippians 2:4). This provides real joy.

THE TAKEAWAY

Every choice we make is an act of worship to someone, whether God or not. We must therefore be very intentional about what we feed our minds and our mouths, as our daily choices will impact the output of our lives—character—and our characters will determine our final destination on this journey.

LIVE JOYFULLY ...

"... he shall not ... remember the days of his life; because God answereth him in the joy of his heart." (Ecclesiastes 5:20 - KJV).

Cake Topper

"Live joyfully with the wife whom thou lovest all the days of the life of thy vanity, which he hath given thee under the sun, all the days of thy vanity: for that is thy portion in this life, and in thy labour which thou takest under the sun." (Ecclesiastes 9:9 - KJV).

DID YOU KNOW?

- Sweet treats had been a part of nuptial feasts for centuries, but Queen Victoria's tiered white cake took the tradition to new heights.

- By the nineteenth century, cake at wedding celebrations was nothing new, but the 1840 wedding of Queen Victoria and Prince Albert took this old tradition and turned it into something new. Their cake was big: three tiers of English plum cake that stood 14 inches tall, measured nearly 10 feet across and weighed 300 pounds.

- Adding to the spectacle (and height) was one of the world's first cake toppers. Victoria and Albert's cake featured several miniature statues, including Britannia, a female personification of Great Britain, on top, blessing the royal couple clad in Roman costume. It soon became popular for small figurines of a bride and groom to appear on top of the wedding cakes of ordinary people.[23]

This study is about marriage and the family.

---

[23] "Queen Victoria's 300-pound wedding cake set a big new trend for brides", June 10, 2021, https://www.nationalgeographic.com/history/history-magazine/article/queen-victoria-wedding-cake-300-pounds-new-trends-brides

1. Where did marriage come from?

"Now the LORD God said, "It is not good (beneficial) for the man to be alone; I will make him a helper [one who balances him—a counterpart who is] suitable and complementary for him." (Genesis 2:18 -AMP).

Marriage was established by God in Eden as a union between a man and a woman. Eve was made from a bone from Adam's side (see Genesis 2:21), symbolising the equality and care they were to show each other. They were meant to be equal partners in the union. Adam was asked to respect Eve as the weaker partner, while remembering that the two were considered heirs together of the gracious gift of life (see 1 Peter 3:7).

2. What was God's plan for marriage and the family?

"Therefore a man shall leave his father and mother and be joined to his wife, and they shall become one flesh." (Genesis 2:24 - NKJV).

God designed marriage and the family to give humanity a glimpse of His heart. These gifts were a window through which humanity could look to understand Him better. When marriage is done right, and a husband and wife experience true oneness and unity—the "two" really do become "one"—then they can begin to understand in a small way how the "three" members of the Godhead are "one."

3. How long was marriage expected to last?

"Therefore what God has joined together, let not man separate." (Mark 10:9 - NKJV).

God expects marriage vows to last for the lifetime of the man and the woman in the union. This design reserves the sacredness of intimacy for a lifelong commitment. God designed us to enjoy intimacy within the protection of a marriage covenant (see Hebrews 13:4).

4. What does God use as a symbol of how much He loves us?

" ... as the bridegroom rejoices over the bride, so shall your God rejoice over you." (Isaiah 62:5 - NKJV).

God uses a happy marriage as a symbol of how much He loves us. Seeing people in happy marriages brings joy to God's heart, and He longs to guide each couple in their marriage as well.

5. With what does Paul compare the marriage relationship?

"Husbands, love your wives, just as Christ also loved the church and gave Himself for her. ... Let each one of you in particular so love his own wife as himself, and let the wife see that she respects her husband." (Ephesians 5:25,33 - NKJV).

Paul uses the analogy of the love of a husband for his wife to demonstrate the love Christ has for His church. This respectful relationship filled with love and understanding is God's ideal for marriage.

6. How is God's love for man seen in the family?

" ... Adam lived one hundred and thirty years, and begot a son in his own likeness, after his image, and named him Seth." (Genesis 5:3 - NKJV).

Just as God created Adam and Eve in His own image (see Genesis 1:27), so marital love is expressed in the creation of children made in their parents' image. This teaches us that God's motivation for creating us was love.

7. *How can challenges in marriage and the family be overcome?*

"Love suffers long and is kind; love does not envy; love does not parade itself, is not puffed up; does not behave rudely, does not seek its own, is not provoked, thinks no evil; does not rejoice in iniquity, but rejoices in the truth; bears all things, believes all things, hopes all things, endures all things." (1 Corinthians 13:4-7 - NKJV).

Challenges in marriage and the family are inevitable. Paul shares the principles of how these challenges can be overcome: by showing unconditional love. True love in marriage and the family must be based on Christ's example because God is love (see 1 John 4:7-8).

8. *What are the responsibilities of parents to their children?*

"Train up a child in the way he should go, and when he is old he will not depart from it." (Proverbs 22:6 - NKJV).

"And these words which I command you today shall be in your heart. You shall teach them diligently to your children, and shall talk of them when you sit in your house, when you walk by the way, when you lie down, and when you rise up." (Deuteronomy 6:6-7 - NKJV).

Parents are called to instruct children in the way of the Lord. As preparation for teaching His precepts, God commands that His precepts be hidden in the hearts of the parents. Parents themselves must show interest in the Bible in order to cultivate a love for its study in their children. This will foster an environment where children delight in honouring their father and mother (see Exodus 20:12).

THE LESSON

God designed marriage as a means of expressing His great love for His creation. Jesus blessed the first union in Eden before sin entered Adam and Eve's world. Certainly, no cake-topper can top that! Marriage is therefore expected to last until death or when life on this earth as we know it ends, whichever comes first.

In Ecclesiastes 9:9, Solomon tells his son to live joyfully with his wife and to love his wife for his whole life. This is similar to the counsel given in Proverbs 5:18, *"Let thy fountain be blessed: and rejoice with the wife of thy youth." (KJV)*.

THE TAKEAWAY

A great day is coming when the great marriage supper of the Lamb will be held. The invitation has been sent out to the guests. A blessing awaits all who will attend (see Revelation 19:9). Let's all make a date to be there!

Ancient Sacred Grain

"Because the sentence against an evil work is not executed speedily, therefore the heart of the sons of men is fully set in them to do evil." (Ecclesiastes 8:11 – NKJV).

DID YOU KNOW?

- Quinoa is a unique grain because it contains all nine essential amino acids, making it a complete protein.

- One cup of cooked quinoa provides about 8 grams of protein, along with magnesium, iron, and B vitamins.

- Its mild, nutty flavour makes it an excellent base for salads, stir-fries, or breakfast bowls.

- Quinoa is also gluten-free, making it perfect for those with "autoimmune" conditions.[24]

Hundreds of years ago, the Inca people considered this ancient grain a sacred food.[25] I like to use quinoa as a substitute for rice. Knowing that it's a complete protein is a nice bonus.

This study is about Christ's ministry in the heavenly sanctuary.

---

[24] "Powerful Plant-Based Proteins", Years Restored Weekly Article by Mercy Ballard dated December 26, 2024

[25] "8 Evidence-Based Health Benefits of Quinoa", June 27, 2024
https://www.healthline.com/nutrition/8-health-benefits-quinoa#nutrients

1. *How is the plan of salvation illustrated in the Old Testament?*

"… let them make Me a sanctuary, that I may dwell among them."
(Exodus 25:8 - NKJV).

God used a three-dimensional model called the sanctuary to illustrate the plan of salvation in the Bible. Each component had a symbolic meaning that helped the children of Israel see, experience, and comprehend the plan of salvation.[26] The Tabernacle provided an avenue for God to dwell among His people so they could get to know Him from close range.

2. *Who was the focus of the sanctuary services?*

"These are the feasts of the Lord …" (Leviticus 23:4 - NKJV).

The Old Testament sanctuary services are a representation of the work Christ does for our salvation. There were seven annual feasts in the Hebrew worship calendar: Passover, Unleavened Bread, Firstfruits, Pentecost, Trumpets, Day of Atonement, and Tabernacles (see Leviticus 23). These feasts were shadows of things to come (see Colossians 2:16). Their fulfilment is seen in Christ. Jesus was represented by the sacrificial offerings (see 1 Corinthians 5:7), including the grain offering (see Leviticus 2:4). He is the quinoa of the sanctuary!

3. *Who else was involved in the sanctuary services?*

"Seeing then that we have a great High Priest who has passed through the heavens, Jesus the Son of God, let us hold fast our

---

[26] "Secrets of the Sanctuary", Inside Report, Amazing Facts, https://www.amazingfacts.org/news-and-features/inside-report/magazine/id/10734/t/secrets-of-the-sanctuary

74

confession. For we do not have a High Priest who cannot sympathize with our weaknesses, but was in all points tempted as we are, yet without sin. Let us therefore come boldly to the throne of grace, that we may obtain mercy and find grace to help in time of need." (Hebrews 4:14-16 - NKJV).

In the earthly sanctuary system, the people of God came to the sanctuary to confess their sins. The priests and the high priest functioned as mediators for the people by offering sacrifices to God for themselves and on behalf of the people. Some blood from the animals that were sacrificed was sprinkled in the sanctuary (see Leviticus 16).

Jesus is our High Priest (see Hebrews 7:26-28). When Jesus ascended to heaven in AD 34, he began His high priestly ministry in the sanctuary in heaven, beginning in the Holy Place (see Hebrews 8:1-2).

Once a year, on the Day of Atonement, atonement was made by the High Priest to cleanse the people from their sins (see Leviticus 16:16). The purpose of this ceremony was to bring people into at-one-ment with God (two becoming one). It was a wedding ceremony!

Throughout the Bible, the Day of Atonement was celebrated on *"the seventh month, on the tenth day of the month"* (see Leviticus 16:29).

4. *When did Jesus commence the Day of Atonement ministry?*

"For two thousand three hundred days; then the sanctuary shall be cleansed." (Daniel 8:14 - NKJV).

Through the study of the prophecy in Daniel 8:14, Bible scholars found that this time period represents twenty-three hundred years. According to Daniel 9:25, the beginning of this prophecy would occur when *"the command to restore and build Jerusalem"* was given. This command was given by King Artaxerxes in B.C. 457. Beginning at this date, the end of the prophecy would be in the year 1844 A.D.

In the early 1800s, a group of believers who traced these prophetic lines believed the earth was the sanctuary. They believed the cleansing of the sanctuary would be at the second coming of Jesus Christ. In 1844, the Day of Atonement fell on October 22, 1844. When Jesus didn't come to the earth then, they prayed and went back to study the Scriptures more carefully. They came to the understanding that instead of returning to earth on the Day of Atonement, Jesus began this process in the Most Holy Place. He began the work of cleansing the heavenly sanctuary of all sin (see Malachi 3:1). We are now living in this Day of Atonement period.

   5.   What is Jesus doing on behalf of His people right now?

"He will sit as a refiner and a purifier of silver; He will purify the sons of Levi, and purge them as gold and silver, that they may offer to the Lord an offering in righteousness." (Malachi 3:3 - NKJV).

"Therefore he is able to save completely those who come to God through him, because he always lives to intercede for them." (Hebrews 7:25 – NIV).

God's original purpose for His created beings was for them to be living temples for the indwelling of the Creator (see 1 Corinthians 3:16). Sin affected this plan, but this is once again possible for all who are reborn through the saving grace of Christ (see 2 Corinthians 5:17).

Jesus is working to cleanse His temple (the hearts, minds, motives, and methods of His people) from selfishness, to give us new hearts so that He can write His law of love in our hearts. He desires to seal us with His seal of approval—His righteous character (see Isaiah 61:10)—so that we can live in at-one-ment or harmony with Him forever (see 1 Corinthians 6:17 and 1 John 3:2).

6. What should the people of God be doing in this time of earth's history?

"Create in me a clean heart, O God, and renew a steadfast spirit within me." (Psalm 51:10 - NKJV).

Just like the Biblical Day of Atonement, God's people should be confessing their sins, presenting themselves to Christ for cleansing (see Leviticus 23:27). We should be preparing our hearts for the Holy Spirit to dwell in them (see Psalm 51:11-12). We should be striving to make our hearts right with God and man while preparing for the second coming of Christ (see Psalm 51:17, 19, and 1 John 3:3).

7. What happens after the Day of Atonement?

" … behold, I am coming quickly, and My reward is with Me, to give to every one according to his work." (Revelation 22:12 - NKJV).

The final feast on the Hebrew calendar, which took place after the Day of Atonement, was the Feast of Tabernacles. This was observed as a time of celebration following the deliverance of God's people from bondage (see Leviticus 23:33-43).

After the great tribulation (see Revelation 7:9-14), Jesus will return to earth to claim His bride—those who remain faithful to God—and will usher them into the marriage supper of the Lamb (see Revelation 19).

THE LESSON

Solomon gave us a reminder about human behaviour in Ecclesiastes 8:11. Because sentencing against evil-doing doesn't take place right away and men don't immediately see the results of their evil choices, they keep on doing wrong, foolishly thinking that they will escape God's judgment. The solemn warning is given in Ecclesiastes 8:12-13 that although their days appear long upon the earth, it shall not be well for evil-doers because they do not fear God. Psalm 37:9-10 informs us that evil-doers will be cut off; however, it will be well with those who fear the Lord.

THE TAKEAWAY

The righteous Judge who will preside in the judgment is Jesus Christ (see Acts 17:31), "the source of all being, and the fountain of all law."[27] He is love (see 1 John 4:8), and He is unchanging (see Malachi 3:6 and Hebrews 13:8). The judgment is good news because the Creator will judge the world with righteousness and the people with truth and equity (see Psalm 9:8, Psalm 96:10, 13, and Psalm 98:9).

He is coming to restore His governance to the earth, to govern the world in love, and to heal people in harmony with His law of love. Let's consider the eternal benefits of having a vibrant relationship with Jesus.

---

[27] Ellen G. White, The Great Controversy, pg 479.2

The Golden Elixir

"For there will come a time when your limbs will tremble with age, your strong legs will become weak, and your teeth will be too few to do their work, and there will be blindness too. Then let your lips be tightly closed while eating when your teeth are gone! And you will waken at dawn with the first note of the birds; but you yourself will be deaf and tuneless, with quavering voice. You will be afraid of heights and of falling—a white-haired, withered old man, dragging himself along: without sexual desire, standing at death's door, and nearing his everlasting home as the mourners go along the streets." (Ecclesiastes 12:3-5 - TLB).

DID YOU KNOW?

- June plum, or golden apple as it is typically known across the Caribbean, is a tropical edible fruit with a fibrous pit. Its scientific name is spondias dulcis.

- June plum has a number of health benefits. It is a high source of Vitamin C, which boosts the immune system, helps with wound healing, and slows down aging. A good immune system helps the body fight against bacteria, viruses, and diseases.

- June plum is widely grown and eaten across Asian countries such as Cambodia, Vietnam, Singapore, Indonesia, Malaysia, and Sri Lanka, in a variety of ways.[28]

This study looks at "The Second Coming" of Jesus Christ.

---

[28] "Fruit for thought: June Plum or Golden Apple", January 22, 2022
https://www.caribbeanrecipes.co.uk/post/fruit-for-thought-june-plum-or-golden-apple

1. *What is the second coming?*

"In my Father's house are many mansions: if it were not so, I would have told you. I go to prepare a place for you. And if I go and prepare a place for you, I will come again, and receive you unto myself; that where I am, there ye may be also." (John 14:2-3 - KJV).

The first time Jesus came to earth, He was a baby. After His ministry on earth, crucifixion, and resurrection, He returned to heaven "to prepare a place" for His followers (see John 14:3). The "Second Coming" or "Second Advent" is a reference to the return of Jesus Christ to earth, as described in the Bible in the gospels, Hebrews, Revelation, and many other places.

2. *What will be the manner of Jesus' second coming?*

"... Ye men of Galilee, why stand ye gazing up into heaven? this same Jesus, which is taken up from you into heaven, shall so come in like manner as ye have seen him go into heaven." (Acts 1:11 - KJV).

Immediately after Jesus' ascension (see Acts 1:9), His disciples were reassured by two angels that His return would be personal and literal. The same Jesus whom they saw ascend to heaven will return as He promised in John 14:1-3. His coming will not be a secret, nor will it be a spiritual event. Jesus' second coming will be visible, audible, and global (see Matthew 24:27, 31, and Revelation 1:7).

3. *What does Matthew 24:36 tell us about the timing of Jesus' second coming?*

"But of that day and hour knoweth no man, no, not the angels of heaven, but my Father only." (Matthew 24:36 - KJV).

Just like the flood of Noah's day, the event of the second coming is sure, but the date has not been disclosed. Although we do not know the specific date of Jesus' second coming, we have been given many signs (see Matthew 24:5-29) that can indicate when the season is near (see Matthew 24:32).

4. *How does Jesus describe His second coming in Matthew 24:43?*

"If the owner of the house knew the time when the thief would come, …. he would stay awake and not let the thief break into his house." (Matthew 24:43 - GNT).

Matthew 24:43 likens Jesus' second coming to the arrival of a thief. A successful thief usually catches people off guard. This message is repeated in 1 Thessalonians 5:2, 2 Peter 3:10, Revelation 3:3, and Revelation 16:15. Believers are therefore called to be wary of false prophets and false christs (see Matthew 7:15, Matthew 24:4-5, 11, 24), "be ready" (see Matthew 24:44), "watch and be sober" (see 1 Thessalonians 5:6), make heart preparation (see 2 Peter 3:11), hold fast to the promise of Jesus' return and repent (see Revelation 3:3), and keep wearing their robes of righteousness (see Revelation 16:15).

5. *What will happen to the righteous when Jesus comes?*

"For this we say to you by the word of the Lord, that we who are alive and remain until the coming of the Lord will by no means precede those who are asleep. For the Lord Himself will descend from heaven with a shout, with the voice of an archangel, and with the trumpet of God. And the dead in Christ will rise first. Then we who are alive and remain shall be caught up together with them in the clouds to meet the Lord in the air. And thus we shall always be with the Lord." (1 Thessalonians 4:15-17 - NKJV)

At the second coming, the righteous dead will be resurrected in fulfilment of the promise in 1 Corinthians 15:21-23, and they, along with the living righteous, will be translated—taken to heaven to be with Jesus.

> 6. *What kind of bodies will the righteous receive at the second coming?*

" ... at the last trump ... the dead shall be raised incorruptible, and we shall be changed. For this corruptible must put on incorruption, and this mortal must put on immortality." (1 Corinthians 15:52-53 - KJV).

The righteous will receive new bodies when Jesus returns. These are described as incorruptible—free from the power of death. Only then will they receive immortality.

THE LESSON

In Ecclesiastes 12:3-5, the Preacher poetically describes some of the natural consequences of aging, such as a feeble body, decaying teeth, and failing eyesight. In Ecclesiastes 12:6-7 he counsels the young to remember the Creator before the silver cord of life snaps and the gold bowl is broken; before the pitcher is broken at the fountain and the wheel is broken at the cistern; when the dust returns to the earth as it was, and the spirit returns to God who gave it. These are all metaphors for death.

THE TAKEAWAY

While elixirs of youth, such as delicious golden apple juice, may boost the immune system, fight disease, and slow the effects of aging, physical decline is one natural consequence of living in a world of sin. The only way to guarantee a reversal of this condition and to get a body that will no longer be subject to death is to get to know and love the Creator now while there is time, and to follow His counsel (see Ecclesiastes 12:13).

Bitter Sweet

"For the living know that they will die; but the dead know nothing, and they have no more reward, For the memory of them is forgotten. Also their love, their hatred, and their envy have now perished; Nevermore will they have a share In anything done under the sun." (Ecclesiastes 9:5-6 - NKJV).

DID YOU KNOW?

- The june plum fruit is made into preserves and provides flavourings for sauces, soups, and stews.

- In Trinidad and Tobago, it is curried, sweetened, salted, or flavoured with pepper sauce and spices.

- In Suriname and Guyana, the fruit is dried and made into a spicy chutney, mixed with garlic and peppers.

- It can be eaten with salt or made into a drink sweetened with sugar and spiced with ginger.[29]

- This juice drink is not only refreshing and tasty, but also packed with nutritional benefits. It is full of Vitamins A, C and K, and rich in calcium, iron, and antioxidants.[30]

The point about the delicious, refreshing june plum drink, sweetened with sugar and spiced with ginger, is certainly true about

---

[29] "Fruit for thought: June Plum or Golden Apple", January 22, 2022
https://www.caribbeanrecipes.co.uk/post/fruit-for-thought-june-plum-or-golden-apple

[30] "June Plum (Golden Apple) Juice Drink", January 22, 2022
https://www.caribbeanrecipes.co.uk/post/june-plum-golden-apple-juice-drink

Jamaica. Ginger is a must-have ingredient for almost all Jamaican fruit juices! Another topic that is rife with Jamaican traditions is that of death and dying.

This study is about the grave topic of death, the state of the dead, and resurrection.

1. *How does the Bible define death?*

"Then the dust will return to the earth as it was, and the spirit will return to God who gave it." (Ecclesiastes 12:7 - NKJV).

When God created man, He breathed the breath of life into Adam's body, and his clay form came to life (see Genesis 2:7). In Ecclesiastes 12:7, Solomon spoke of the reverse, *"Then the dust will return to the earth as it was, and the spirit will return to God who gave it." (NKJV).*

Death may be defined as the absence of life. Think of an electric light source. If you take away the power supply, you are left with the lightbulb. It may feel warm for a while, but given enough time, it will grow cold and will be useless unless the power returns.

2. *Why does death exist?*

"For the wages of sin is death, but the gift of God is eternal life in Christ Jesus our Lord." (Romans 6:23 - NKJV).

When Adam and Eve chose to listen to the serpent's lie in Eden (see Genesis 3:4) rather than to God (see Genesis 2:17) and to eat from the Tree of the Knowledge of Good and Evil, they sinned (see James 4:17). As a result, they lost their conditional immortality and became subject to death. It was just a matter of time before their power went out. Adam died at the grand age of 930 years (see

Genesis 5:5). The rest of the human family also became subject to death as a result of Adam's disobedience (see Romans 5:12, 19).

3. *Why didn't Adam and Eve die immediately after they sinned?*

"... the Lamb slain from the foundation of the world." (Revelation 13:8 - NKJV).

When Adam and Eve sinned, they didn't experience physical death at once, but love and trust died. They started to blame each other, God, and the serpent for their act of rebellion against God and His law of love (see Genesis 3:12-13). Their close connection to God was severed in the process, and they began to experience selfishness and fear (see Genesis 3:10).

The Godhead immediately activated the plan of salvation, which had been put in place before the world was created. Jesus, the Lamb slain from the foundation of the world, stepped in and gave the assurance that He would take our terminal condition upon Himself (see 1 Peter 2:24) and provide the remedy for their sin. Symbolically, an animal was sacrificed, and its skin was used to cover their nakedness (see Genesis 3:7,21).

4. *How does the Bible explain the state of the dead?*

"… He said to them, "Our friend Lazarus sleeps, but I go that I may wake him up. Then His disciples said, "Lord, if he sleeps he will get well." However, Jesus spoke of his death, but they thought that He was speaking about taking rest in sleep. Then Jesus said to them plainly, "Lazarus is dead."" (John 11:11-14 - NKJV).

In numerous places throughout the Bible, the dead are declared to be asleep. Take three kings of old who died and were buried. *"So*

David slept with his fathers and was buried ..." (see 1 Kings 2:10). "And Solomon slept with his fathers, and was buried ..." (see 1 Kings 11:43). "And Rehoboam slept with his fathers, and was buried ..." (see 1 Kings 14:31). These kings who had all died were described as being asleep.

When Jesus received the message from Mary and Martha that their brother Lazarus was sick and the request to come and heal him, he waited for four days before making the journey to their house. He explained to His disciples that He was going to wake Lazarus from the sleep of death.

> 5. Why is a proper understanding of the state of the dead important?

"Then the serpent said to the woman, "You will not surely die.""
(Genesis 3:4 - NKJV).

Satan tricked Eve into believing a lie about the consequence of sinning against God. He implied that it was acceptable to disobey God and live forever, while being out of harmony with God's principles and His law of love. Believing this lie lulls individuals into feeling comfortable while living in a state of rebellion against God (see Ecclesiastes 8:11).

Another danger arises from not understanding that death is a state of unconscious sleep; Satan and his fallen angels can transform themselves into angels of light (see 2 Corinthians 11:14-15) and seek to impersonate family members and friends who have died. Their primary goal is to deliver false messages, which are supposedly from God (see the story of King Samuel and the medium of En-dor in 1 Samuel 28). For this reason, God has always warned against the practice of attempting to communicate with familiar spirits and with the dead (necromancy) (see Deuteronomy 18:11).

6. When will the resurrection of the righteous take place?

"Do not marvel at this; for the hour is coming in which all who are in the graves will hear His voice and come forth—those who have done good, to the resurrection of life, and those who have done evil, to the resurrection of condemnation." (John 5:28-29 - NKJV).

Jesus makes the distinction between the resurrection of life (first resurrection) and the resurrection of condemnation (second resurrection).

THE FIRST RESURRECTION

The first resurrection is the resurrection of the righteous dead and leads to everlasting life. Those who will heed Jesus' Word and believe in the Father who sent Him on a rescue mission to earth (see John 3:16) will be raised first. The first resurrection will take place *"at the last day"* (see John 6:40), when Jesus returns for His faithful people (see 1 Corinthians 15:52). The righteous dead will sleep in their graves until then.

During her discourse with Jesus about Lazarus, Martha indicated that she understood the state of the dead correctly when she said: *"I know that he will rise again in the resurrection at the last day." (John 11:24 - NKJV).* She understood this to mean that Lazarus was dead and awaiting the first resurrection.

THE SECOND RESURRECTION

When Jesus comes the second time, "at the last day", unrighteous people who are <u>alive</u> will die (see 2 Thessalonians 2:7-8), and the unrighteous <u>dead</u> will remain asleep in their graves. The second resurrection is the resurrection (awaking) of all the unrighteous dead to receive the wages of their sin and selfishness (see Romans 6:23 (KJV) – *"... the wages of sin is death ..."*). There is no resurrection from this death. It is called the second death.

7. When will the resurrection of the unrighteous take place?

"(The rest of the dead did not come to life until the thousand years were over.)" (Revelation 20:5 - GNT).

The resurrection of the unrighteous dead *("the rest of the dead")* will take place at the second resurrection—after the millennium. The millennium is a period of 1000 years following the first resurrection. We will explore this topic further in the next lesson.

THE LESSON

In Ecclesiastes 9:5-6, Solomon nailed home the point that those who die the first death will rest in a state of sleep until they are resurrected by Jesus. While in that sleep, they will be unconscious—totally unaware of what is happening in this world after they die.

The first death is not the end of all things. Everyone who dies the first death will be resurrected, some to live forever with Jesus, and some to die the second death from which there is no resurrection.

THE TAKEAWAY

We need to make time to live for Jesus now. The characters that we develop here on earth will be preserved by God and will determine whether we wake up in the first or second resurrection (see Ecclesiastes 3:17).

The Bitter End

"For God will bring every deed into judgment, with every secret thing, whether good or evil." (Ecclesiastes 12:14 - ESV).

Diseases and death are two of the consequences of living in a world of sin. Since Eden, humanity has been looking high and low for ways to change this situation.

DID YOU KNOW?

- June plum contains iron and traces of Vitamin B1, which are important components for the formation of red blood cells that increases the flow of oxygen around the body. This means it can help prevent anaemia.

- Recent studies have shown that it can reduce hypertension (high blood pressure) due to the high concentration of nutrients like vitamin C and minerals like magnesium, potassium, and calcium, along with other compounds present in the fruit.[31]

I went to the doctor to discuss some test results, and she recommended that I do a blood profile test—also known as a complete blood count (CBC). Blood count tests measure the number and types of cells in your blood and help doctors check on your overall health. They can also help to diagnose diseases and conditions such as anaemia, infections, clotting problems, blood cancers, and immune system disorders.[32]

---

[31] "Fruit for thought: June Plum or Golden Apple", January 22, 2022 https://www.caribbeanrecipes.co.uk/post/fruit-for-thought-june-plum-or-golden-apple

[32] "Blood Count Tests", https://medlineplus.gov/bloodcounttests.html

This study is about the millennium and the elusive, highly anticipated end of sin.

1. *What is the millennium?*

...They came to life and ruled as kings with Christ for a thousand years. (The rest of the dead did not come to life until the thousand years were over.) This is the first raising of the dead. (Revelation 20:4-5 - GNT).

The millennium is the thousand-year period that begins with the resurrection of the righteous (the first resurrection) and ends with the resurrection of the unrighteous (the second resurrection). Where you spend the millennium depends on which group you fall within.

2. *Where will the righteous be during the millennium?*

"Happy and greatly blessed are those who are included in this first raising of the dead. The second death has no power over them; they shall be priests of God and of Christ, and they will rule with him for a thousand years." (Revelation 20:6 - GNT).

The righteous will spend the millennium in heaven with Christ and his angels.

3. *Where will Satan be during the millennium?*

"... an angel coming down from heaven, holding in his hand the key of the abyss and a heavy chain. ... seized ... Satan—and chained him up for a thousand years. The angel threw him into the abyss, locked it, and sealed it, so that he could not deceive the nations any more until the thousand years were over. After that he must be set loose for a little while." (Revelation 20:1-3 - GNT).

During the millennium, Satan will be bound to the earth, not with a physical chain but a symbolic, figurative one. Since all the righteous will be in heaven with Christ, and the unrighteous will all be fast asleep (dead) on earth, he will not have anyone to deceive for the thousand-year period. This will be a time of great distress for him.

4. *Where will the unrighteous be during the millennium?*

"(The rest of the dead did not come to life until the thousand years were over)." (Revelation 20:5 - GNT).

The unrighteous dead will continue to sleep in their graves on earth during the millennium.

5. *What will the righteous people of God be doing during the millennium?*

"Don't you know that God's people will judge the world? ... Do you not know that we shall judge the angels?" (1 Corinthians 6:2-3 - GNT).

During the millennium, the righteous will take part in the judgment of all who are lost, including the devil and his angels (see 1 Corinthians 6:2-3). The judgment of the unrighteous will be based on the fruit of their lives on earth (see Matthew 12:31-37). Since they will be dead during the judgment, it is their life records that will be scrutinised (see Revelation 20:12-13).

6. *What will happen after the millennium?*

"For yet a little while and the wicked shall be no more; Indeed, you will look carefully for his place, but it shall be no more." (Psalm 37:10 - NKJV).

Christ will come from heaven to earth for the third time at the end of the millennium. He will be accompanied by the righteous and the angels of heaven. Then the second resurrection will take place. The unrighteous dead from all nations on earth will be raised to life. Satan will make one last attempt to deceive the wicked. His final lie will be to trick them into believing that they can attack the righteous people of God and win. They will try, but they will fail miserably (see Revelation 20:7-9).

The unrighteous will be unable to live in the glorious and righteous presence of God (see Isaiah 33:14). ***"And the devil who had deceived them was hurled into the lake of fire and burning brimstone (sulfur), where the beast (Antichrist) and false prophet are also; and they will be tormented day and night, forever and ever." (Revelation 20:10 – AMP).*** The unrighteous will all perish (see John 3:16 and Malachi 4:1). This is the experience of the second death.

"Then death and Hades [the realm of the dead] were thrown into the lake of fire. This is the second death, the lake of fire [the eternal separation from God]" (Revelation 20:14 – AMP) in fulfilment of the prophecy in Isaiah 25:8.

THE LESSON

In Ecclesiastes 12:14, Solomon reminds us that no one will be able to hide their heart's true condition from God, whether healed by the remedy Jesus provides or still deceitful and desperately wicked (see Jeremiah 17:9). Our choices today all have consequences and will determine our reward when Jesus returns (see Revelation 22:11-12).

Satan, the originator of every sin, and every evil-doer in his army will be utterly cut off (see Psalm 37:9). This will be the end of sin and all its ugly consequences (see Nahum 1:9).

THE TAKEAWAY

Those who give their allegiance to Satan and do not partake of the healing remedy that Christ offers—so that their characters may be restored to Christlikeness and their names written in the Book of Life—will be thrown into the lake of God's fiery presence, where truth and love will consume all lies, deceit, and selfishness.

"For evildoers shall be cut off, but those who wait and hope and look for the Lord [in the end] shall inherit the earth." (Psalm 37:9 – AMPC).

A Taste of Paradise

"Truly the light is sweet, and a pleasant thing it is for the eyes to behold the sun." (Ecclesiastes 11:7 - KJV).

DID YOU KNOW?

- The june plum is dynamic. It may be peeled and eaten, stewed or juiced. The flesh is crunchy and a little sour when green. When it is fully ripe, it turns yellow or golden in colour (hence the name golden apple) and takes on a pineapple-mango flavour. In Thai cuisine, both the fruits and the tender leaves are eaten.

- It has antibiotic properties that help the body fight against bacteria and infections caused by bacteria.

- It is also a good source of Vitamin A and Vitamin K, which are good natural antioxidants. Antioxidants reduce or neutralise free radicals that may damage the eye lens, which leads to vision loss, arthritis (inflammation of the joints), damage to nerve cells in the brain, and activate cancer cells.[33]

My childhood memories include savouring the biggest, ripest golden apples you could find for miles around. As children, my younger siblings and I looked forward to the days when our neighbour would bring us bags containing at least one dozen of this most delicious fruit. Little did I know of the many health benefits they provided.

---

[33] "Fruit for thought: June Plum or Golden Apple", January 22, 2022, https://www.caribbeanrecipes.co.uk/post/fruit-for-thought-june-plum-or-golden-apple

This study deals with the new earth, a place where there will be no more disease. Let's dig in.

1. *Where will the redeemed spend eternity?*

"Nevertheless we, according to His promise, look for new heavens and a new earth in which righteousness dwells." (2 Peter 3:13 - NKJV).

A resounding theme of the Scriptures is "God With Us." It is echoed throughout Scripture, from Genesis to Revelation. It started when God met to fellowship with Adam and Eve in the cool of the day, before they were expelled from Eden (see Genesis 3:8). Afterward, God made an earthly sanctuary (see Exodus 25:8), and Isaiah foretold that the coming Messiah would be called Immanuel, meaning, "God With Us" (see Isaiah 7:14). Finally, in Revelation.

"Behold, the tabernacle of God is with men, and he will dwell with them, and they shall be his people, and God himself shall be with them, and be their God." (Revelation 21:3 – KJV).

2. *What will be the condition of the new earth?*

"And I saw a new heaven and a new earth: for the first heaven and the first earth were passed away ... And he that sat upon the throne said, Behold, I make all things new. ..." (Revelation 21:1, 5 - KJV).

The fire that will consume the wicked will also purify the earth. Every trace of sin's curse will be removed.

3. *What will life in the new earth be like?*

"And God shall wipe away all tears from their eyes; and there shall be no more death, neither sorrow, nor crying, neither shall there be any more pain: for the former things are passed away." (Revelation 21:4 - KJV).

All tears will be dried, mourning will turn to rejoicing, sorrow will be replaced with joy, painful memories will be erased, and praises will ascend to God through eternity (see Isaiah 35:10 and Isaiah 51:11). There will be perfect harmony between all the inhabitants of the new earth, human, angelic and divine.

4. *Who will be the source of healing in the new earth?*

"But unto you that fear my name shall the Sun of righteousness arise with healing in his wings; and ye shall go forth, and grow up as calves of the stall." (Malachi 4:2 - KJV).

Jesus, the great Physician, offers complete healing and restoration. Isaiah prophesied: *"Behold, your God will come; ... he will come and save you. Then the eyes of the blind shall be opened, and the ears of the deaf shall be unstopped." (Isaiah 35:4-5 – KJV).*

5. *What will be included in the diet of the redeemed in the new earth?*

"And he shewed me a pure river of water of life, clear as crystal, proceeding out of the throne of God and of the Lamb. In the midst of the street of it, and on either side of the river, was there the tree of life, which bare twelve manner of fruits, and yielded her fruit every month: and the leaves of the tree were for the healing of the nations." (Revelation 22:1-2 - KJV).

The redeemed will eat fruit and healing leaves from the *Tree of Life, which is in the midst of the paradise of God* (see Revelation 2:7).

THE LESSON

Sunlight is a key component needed to ripen fruit and bring out its inherent sweet taste. It is also especially important for persons with certain health challenges—for example, cancer, cataracts, depression, and fibroids—to get an adequate supply daily.

Solomon observed in Ecclesiastes 11:7 that natural light is sweet, and being able to see the sun gives pleasure. He was grateful for the gift of life and the ability to see and enjoy his surroundings, including the relationships with his beloved.

God's original plan to dwell in harmony and close fellowship with humanity will be restored in the new earth—where the redeemed people of God from all ages will spend eternity with Christ, the Desire of Ages (see Haggai 2:7).

THE TAKEAWAY

The signs of the time—such as scoffers in the last days who deny the flood and say, "Christ is not coming" (see 2 Peter 3:3-6)—confirm that the fulfilment of this promise is near. Let us anchor our faith in the more sure word of Bible prophecy and *"grow in grace, and in the knowledge of our Lord and Saviour Jesus Christ"* that we may be found of Him in peace, without spot, and blameless (see 2 Peter 1:19, 3:14, 18).

ABOUT THE AUTHOR

Colette Guthrie is a dedicated Christian who loves to study the Word of God. Her interest in Bible study was born when she attended Sunday School at the local neighbourhood church as a child. Baby steps on her journey of faith led her to attend the Inter Schools Christian Fellowship (ISCF) group on the campus of the high school where she first accepted Jesus Christ as her personal saviour.

Her search for truth led her to search the Scriptures. She became a member of the Seventh-day Adventist Church as an adult. She currently volunteers as an adult Sabbath School Teacher at the Linstead Seventh-day Adventist Church.

Colette has led several online small group Bible study sessions with church members and friends over the years. She loves to memorize Scripture and to share her love for the Word of God and the God of the Word with those around her.

To connect with Colette, visit her website at https://thoughtstothewise.com and follow her on IG, FB, and LinkedIn.

Email: info@thoughtstothewise.com to join her mailing list.

www.ingramcontent.com/pod-product-compliance
Lightning Source LLC
LaVergne TN
LVHW051811080426
835513LV00017B/1909